The New Acropolis Museum

monuments and men

1st publication June 2009

TRANSLATION FROM GREEK ELENI ANTONOPOULOU
EDITOR FOTINI XIFARA
DESIGN EVDOKIA STIVAKTAKI

ISBN 978-960-455-612-0
AUXIL. COMPU. CODE 4612
C.E.P. 1777, C.P. 1975

MετаιCHMIO 🕀

Bookstores
1. 18 ASKLIPIOU STR., 106 80 ATHENS
    TEL.: +30 210 3647 433, FAX: +30 211 3003562
    Internet Site: www.metaixmio.gr
    e-mail: metaixmio@metaixmio.gr
2. POLYCHOROS, IPPOKRATOUS 118, 114 72 ATHENS
    TEL.: +30 211 3003580, FAX: +30 211 3003581
3. OLYMPOU 81, 546 31 THESSALONIKI
    TEL.: +30 2310 250075, 2310 260085, FAX: +30 2310 260085

ISO 9001
ΕΣΥΔ
No 110
EN 45012
ACCREDITED
CERT
Quality Assurance ISO 9001

QMSCERT® No 04/1230/279
QMSCERT® No 04/1230/279.1

MARISA DE CASTRO

The New Acropolis Museum

monuments and men

a guide for young people

on the book and the New Museum
PANOS VALAVANIS
MICHALIS PHOTIADIS

METAICHMIO

A FEW WORDS ON THE BOOK AND THE NEW MUSEUM

Museums are schools. They are actually the most appropriate environment for the reception of History. Their doors, their gates, or their Propylaia, provide the ideal gateway for students to enter the ancient world. This is especially true of the Acropolis and its New Museum within which a world of magic opens up before our eyes: from the archaic pediments to the Moschoforos, the Korai, the Boy of Kritias, the Blond Ephebos, the architectural sculptures of the Ionic temples, the Karyatides and, above all, the singular sculptures of the Parthenon!

Works of unique conception and execution, unrivalled sculptures and monuments – both aesthetically pleasing and artistically expressive– are waiting for us to observe them with our senses, to enjoy them with our feelings and to cherish them with our souls. But it is not only this that awaits us; it is also the exploration of an important political and historical era. The enjoyment of knowledge is combined with the pleasure of beauty and the delight of uniqueness. A visit to the New Acropolis Museum will reveal the multiple aspects of ancient Greek artistic creation while encouraging an exploration of the beneficial role of great art in shaping the soul of humanity and inspiring the young human being.

Yet, although modern exhibitions are instructive, there is always the need for a "guide"; a link between the past and the present. Marisa de Castro plays this part masterfully. Based on her long experience and knowledge of the principles of Museum Education, she takes children by the hand and guides them through the rooms of the large museum, and with her they are never lost in the labyrinth of artworks. A master of the secret teacher recipes, she knows where to stop and explore, which pieces require special attention and which elements need to be highlighted in order to captivate and fascinate.

The New Acropolis Museum: Monuments and Men is an educational tool that intends to inspire teachers and students, helping them understand and enjoy the works produced by a handful of Greeks in an important historical period: a period in which the Greek world had the progress and ennoblement of people at its heart – just like the book itself.

Panos Valavanis
Professor of Classical Archaeology
University of Athens

on the Acropolis

the Acropolis
in Ancient Times

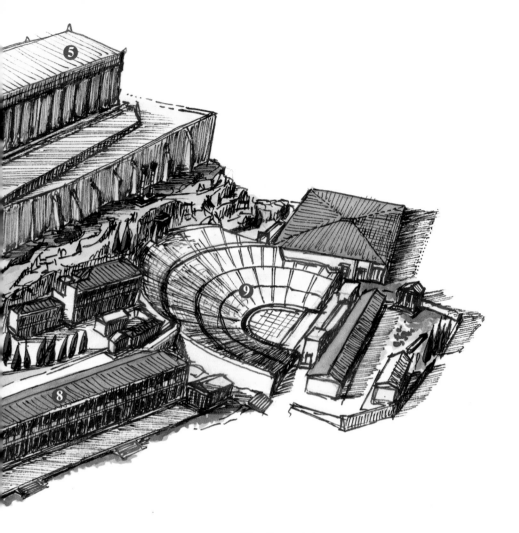

1. The Propylaia
2. The Pinakotheke
3. The Temple of Athena Nike
4. The Vravronion
5. The Parthenon
6. The Erechtheion
7. The Odeion of Herodes Atticus
8. The Stoa of Eumenes
9. The Theatre of Dionysos

the Acropolis

4,000 years before the birth of Christ, people built small homes on the tallest **hill** of an area that was later to be called Athens. The hill is a natural fort: **steep** on three sides with only one approach on the west. Wide and even on the top, it was ideal for construction with fresh **water springs** on the south slope. In the Mycenaean era, a circuit wall –called the **Cyclopean wall**– was built around the city to protect it from enemies. It was also in this era that a palace was built for the reigning king.

During the Geometric and Archaic times, the city at the foot of the hill expanded. The **Acropolis** –the **highest point** of that city– grew from fortress to **religious centre** when the Athenians built the old temple of the goddess Athena there. Soon after 500 BC, the Theatre of Dionysos was constructed on the south slope of this "sacred rock".

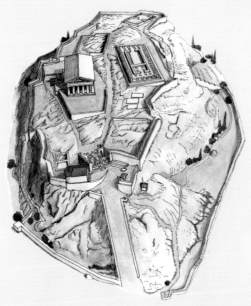

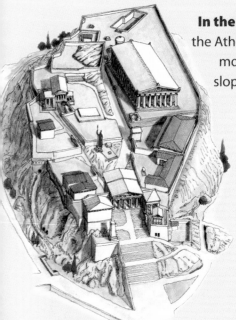

In the Classical period –after the Persian wars– the Athenians rebuilt the whole site and erected the monuments which you see today. On the south slope they built the **Odeion of Perikles** and the **Asklepieion** –the sanctuary of the god of medicine– near the spring from which water still flows to this day.

Later, **in the Hellenistic era**, the **Stoa of Eumenes** was constructed. The **Odeion of Herodes Atticus** was built in Roman times.

The monuments that we see here **today** are those which have survived **heavy destruction** over many centuries.

a natural fort

entering the

The drums of the columns fit perfectly together, one on top of the other, without any binding material between them. In their centre, both on the top and the bottom, they have a square hole for the empolion – a piece of hard wood. It was with the help of this piece of wood that the builders were able to turn the drums around until they found the perfect fit.

Acropolis

When Perikles, as head of the Athenian state –and supporter of arts–
commissioned the architect **Mnesikles** to construct the **Propylaia**,
they both envisaged a majestic gateway to the Acropolis.

The six heavy **Doric columns** at the façade of the Propylaia are still in place
as are the **Ionian** ones inside. The paved passages
between the columns have also survived to the present day,
but the roof has collapsed.
In actual fact, the construction of the Propylaia was never completed!
How do we know?

We know because a number of ancient authors **wrote** about it...
Construction started in 437 BC, not long before the **Peloponnesian war**.
When war broke out in 431 BC, the Athenians had more immediate needs
to attend to and therefore could not afford the completion
of such a big building.

But we have evidence too...
If we go through the Propylaia, turn right towards the temple of Athena Nike
and look at the back walls of the Propylaia, we can see **lifting bosses** sticking out
of the marble building **blocks**. Those bosses were like handles. Appearing on both
sides of each block they allowed the workers to secure the marble in place.
Workers would drive **ropes** through the bosses
and lift the blocks with **cranes** to put them in position.
It was then the **stone carver's** job to chisel the bosses
smoothing the surfaces of the wall.

When **building** stopped because of the war,
no one bothered to smooth off the surfaces
of the back walls.

Pausanias, the travel-writer, noted: "To the right of the Parthenon there is a temple of wingless Nike. From that spot you can see the sea and it is said that this is the place from which Aegeus jumped and committed suicide". Do you remember the myth? Theseus agreed with his father –Aegeus– that he would use white sails if returning alive from his encounter with the Minotaur in Crete. But Theseus, forgetting the agreement, left the black sails on. When his father saw the boat he jumped to his death.

Athena Nike

Goddess Athena was worshipped for her many different roles:
She was called
Promachos for **leading** the troops in battle
Polias for **protecting** the city
Ergane for **protecting work**
Hygieia for **giving health** and caring for the sick
Nike for **securing** victory to the Athenians.

In 421 BC, the Athenians started building a small temple on the Acropolis
– dedicated to Athena Nike. Here, they worshipped Athena as a **wingless goddess**: unlike the winged goddess Nike who **could fly** and **give victory** to whoever deserved it, wingless Athena stayed by the Athenians side, securing victory for them at all times.

The temple of Athena Nike was destroyed and restored 3 times in its long history. It was first dismantled by the Ottoman Turks in 1687, so that the stones could be used to support a rampart they built during the war with the Venetians. It was restored for the first time when Athens became the capital of the Greek state and once again in 1923.

In 1975 the decision was made to restore and
reconstruct **all** the monuments on the Acropolis.
This was the beginning of a new adventure for the small temple of Athena!
In 2000, it was dismantled for the third time. All 300 pieces of stone were taken away for restoration.
The rusty iron **clamps** of the stones were **replaced** with new titanium ones, missing parts were **restored**, those stones which had been misplaced in earlier restorations were **put into the right place**, the reliefs of the friezes were **cleaned** from the effects of pollution and replaced by plaster **cast copies**.
For many years, a huge **restoration programme** has been in progress on the Acropolis to **treat the damage** sustained by the monuments.

from the quarry

Workers used to swarm the sacred rock of the Acropolis
setting up scaffolding, carrying materials, carving marble, taking measurements,
discussing and making decisions with foremen... and always keeping a look out
for new loads from the quarry.

On the **west slope** of the rock, where access is relatively easy,
they have constructed a flagstone ramp 20m wide and 80m long.
They used this ramp to enable the sledges to deliver the roughly cut
marble blocks from the quarry on mount Pentelikon to the Acropolis.
Excess marble was cut away at the quarry **to reduce** the weight of the blocks.
The stone was cut to the required size,
following precise instructions from the architects.

In the summer months, when the roads were dry,
15 wagons carried marble to the Acropolis every day.

The stone was transported with great care.
Ten pairs of mules were needed to pull each wagon. They had to be well fed
and **well rested**. The ropes had to be strong and securely tied
in order to keep the stone on the sledge.

to the worksite

The toughest and most tiring part of the journey
was from the foot of the rock to the worksite,
on the ramp going uphill. At the **highest point** of that ramp,
stood a **huge pulley** with very thick ropes. When everything was ready and the
signal was given, they used this device to pull the marble blocks up.
The loaded wagon would then slowly slide up to the Propylon
–the entrance to the Acropolis– as the mules
went down the ramp pulling in the opposite direction.

When the marble reached the top, sledges sliding on wooden
tracks were used to deliver it to the masons and craftsmen.

the Parthenon

Commencement of construction: 447 BC
Duration of construction: 9 years
Inauguration: 438 BC
Architects: Iktinos and Kallikrates
Sculptors: Pheidias and his apprentices
Material: Pentelic marble
Columns: Doric order, 17 on each long side and 8 on each narrow side
Height of columns: 10.43m
Metopes[1]: 92
Frieze[2] : 160m

When **Perikles** and his **colleagues**
envisaged the majestic temple of their patron goddess Athena, here
on the Acropolis, they could not have imagined that the monument
would still be standing 2,500 years later!

Travellers visiting the Acropolis throughout the centuries have left behind
lengthy descriptions of what they saw.

through

When the time came for the **ancient gods to be forgotten**
and for Athenians to follow the **new religion**, they decided
to convert the Parthenon into a Christian church. And since it had been
home to a virgin goddess –Athena Parthenos– they consecrated it to the
Virgin they now worshipped – **Virgin Mary the Athenian**.
They closed the east entrance to put the sanctuary in its place
and opened a new entrance on the west side.
They also painted Christian murals.

the centuries

Later, soon after 1200 AD,
the **Crusaders** conquered Athens dedicating the church to **Santa Maria**.

In 1456, **Mohamed the Conqueror** entered the city victorious.
The Ottoman Turks swiftly **converted** the large church
on the Acropolis into a **mosque** where they would worship their own God.
A minaret was built nearby for the muezzin to call the faithful to prayer.

Everything changed in 1687 with the war between the Turks
and the Venetians.
The Venetians besieged what they called the **castle of Athens**.
Their commander, Francisco Morosini, set canons around the hill
and bombarded the Acropolis.
The Parthenon was **blown to pieces**.

The temple that had been revered for centuries and had served as a place of
worship for a number of religions was **ruined**. Sculptures and reliefs traveled far,
while the scattered marbles were **used** to build new houses on the hill.

Construction of the Erechtheion was completed in 406 BC. This was the last building of the classical period erected on the Acropolis – and the most complex one. It housed not only a temple of Athena, but also one of Poseidon and a grave for the mythical king Kekrops. The Athenians believed that the Erechtheion was built on the spot where the gods held a contest to decide who should be the protector of the city. It was here, they believed, that the sacred olive tree grew, that Poseidon's trident hit the rock from which water sprang, that the wooden statue of Athena Polias fell from the sky and it was here that the mythical King of Athens, Erechtheus, was worshipped.

workers

Every year the Athenians kept **records** of how much
money had been spent on each project.
Fortunately, certain accounts from the year 407 BC have been **preserved**.
They provide us with the names of those who had **worked** on the Erechtheion,
the **names** of their **workshops**, their **area of expertise** and the **wages** paid to
them.

Expertise of men who worked on the project:
Architect
Project manager
Haulers and coachmen
Rope weavers and wood-workers for the scaffolding
Metalworkers, tool makers
Builders, marble masons for the columns and sculptors for the details
Gilders and painters for the final touches.

and wages

Cost of works
For the frieze

Full-size marble statuettes	60 drachmas
Half-size figure	30 drachmas
Child statuette	20 drachmas

For the columns

Flutes for one column	300 drachmas

Hundreds of craftsmen contributed to the **public works** of the Acropolis. Most
of them were **metics** –resident foreigners– few were **citizens** and fewer still
were **slaves**. Their wages varied. Citizens earned **more**.

in the New
Acropolis Museum

Hesychios –a 5th century AD grammarian from Alexandria– wrote that on the eve of the sea-battle at Salamis, the Athenians saw an owl in flight and thought it an omen: they would beat the Persians!

the owl

When you look at a statue or a composition on a vase or relief, **how** can you tell **who** is being depicted?

You can tell by the age and the clothing of the figure... but the best clues are the symbols they hold in their hands or have beside them.

Winged Cupid –Eros– flies near Aphrodite.
Hephaestus holds the **tools** of his craft.
Artemis has her **quiver**, filled with arrows, hanging from her shoulder.
Dionysos wears a **wreath** of ivy leaves.
And **Athena** is followed by her favourite owl, the bird of wisdom.

At the entrance of the New Museum we find the owl, carved on marble from Paros. It stood, for many years before this, right at the top of the Acropolis rock, welcoming visitors to the old museum.

Athenians know the owl quite well.
The little owl of their goddess nests in **caves** all around the rock, in the **old houses** of Plaka, in **the groves** of Athens hills, in the mountains of Attica...

The ancient Athenians
made use of its **image** on their coins
and, sometimes, they **painted** it on the Panathenaic amphoras[3].
Pheidias **sculpted** it on the **gold-and-ivory** statue of Athena in the Parthenon.

fire

Three human bodies with their snake tails intertwining,
three smiling, bearded **old men**.

The first one holds **lightning**, the symbol of **fire**,
the one in the middle holds water,
the third, who is looking straight at us, holds a **bird** symbolizing **air**.

They called this creature the **Triple-bodied Monster**.
Perhaps it is Nereus –the great sea-god inhabiting the Aegean– protector of
sailors and father of the 50 Nereids.

water

He had the gifts of prophesy and wisdom,
and could **change form** at will
to become **fire**, **water** or **air**. He used these powers against **Herakles** when
asked the secret location of the **Garden of Hesperides** – the garden from which
Herakles had to fetch the golden apples and deliver them to Eurystheus to complete his eleventh super-human challenge.

air

What is he looking at?
He is watching two lions tearing apart a calf and Hercules, who is on the left
of the pediment[4], wrestling with Triton – son of Poseidon and Amphitrete.
Triton was a sea-creature with the body of a human and the tail of a fish.
The scales of his tail are painted blue and red.

The Triple-bodied Monster is made of limestone,
which is softer than marble.
Both beard and hair are painted blue,
the bodies of the snakes are striped blue, red and white.

This composition comes from the pediment of the Hekatompedon
[the earliest Parthenon], built in 540 BC. When the Athenians decided
to rebuild the temples on the Acropolis, which had been destroyed
by the Persians in 480 BC, they buried the damaged statues and sculptures.
The excavations at the end of the 19th century brought them back to light.

Gorgon

No need to be afraid! The marble head of Medusa with her deadly eyes
has lost its power! She was killed by Perseus who offered her head to Athena.
The goddess put it on her shield to scare off enemies. According to another myth,
Medusa's blood had magical properties: if it ran from her left side,
it was poisonous; if it ran from the right, it could bring the dead back to life.
Perseus collected the blood in two vials and gave the good blood to Asklepios,
the god of medicine and healing, and the poisonous blood to Athena
to use against her enemies.

Archaeologists **guess** that the head of the Gorgon Medusa was the akroterion
–the sculptured figure placed on the corner of a roof–
of Hekatombedon, an old Acropolis temple.
Why would they put a monster's head there?
Perhaps it was meant to frighten those who were disrespectful to the goddess.

Far away in the west, even further than the **Garden of Hesperides**
and the Kingdom of the Dead, there lived three sisters: Stheno, Euryale
and **Medusa**.
No one dared approach their land. The rocks at the end of the earth,
where they lived, were **scattered** with carcasses. And whoever dared talk about
the sisters, god or mortal, had nothing but **horror stories to tell**.
They were horrifying **to look at**!
Serpents grew from their heads instead of hair, **wild boar's teeth** shot out of
their mouths, no one could escape if caught in their **copper hands** and
no creature could fly faster than they did when flapping their **golden wings**.
The two elder sisters were immortal, but Medusa, the youngest, was not.
She had an **invincible weapon**, though. Her eyes!

a monster that makes your blood curdle

Her **eyes** were so penetrating that they could **turn to stone** anyone who dared
look at her!
The myth says:
Medusa was a beautiful girl with wonderful, long hair.
But one day she **boasted** that her beauty surpassed that
of the **goddess Athena**.
The goddess was furious and turned her into a **monster**...

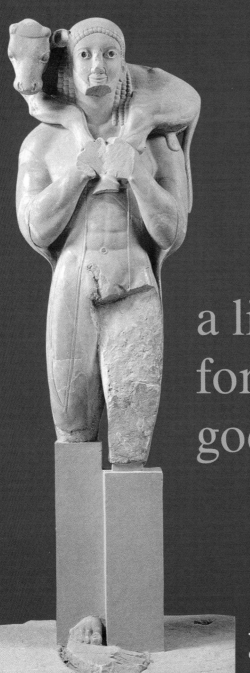

a little calf for the goddess

The shape of my body forms a letter.
Can you work out which one?

They found me in a pit on the Acropolis along with many other statues.
I **carry** a calf, so they called me **Moschoforos**, the **calf-bearer**.
The calf is leaning his **head** on my shoulder, ever so gently. I can feel his
breath on my face. His **tail** is resting on my arm.

The marble I am sculpted on has been dug up from the pit-mines of mount
Hymettus. **Hymettus** is very close to Athens, so it was not too tiring to cart the
marble to the workshop.

Take a closer look at my head.
My **hair** is long and curly. I wear a hair-band to prevent it from
falling into my eyes. The hair-band may have been **painted**...
My **eyes** are large and they are expressive even without pupils.
I am **smiling softly**, perhaps to show that the man who offered
this statue of me to the goddess was happy with his act.
I have a **beard**, which shows that I am a grown man.
Despite that, I resemble a **kouros** – a statue of a young man.
Like those figures, I am standing upright and making a **little step**
forward with my left foot. It is with this step, and the smile,
that the sculptor made me look alive!
I have a short cloak on my shoulders, a **himation**[5].

I wonder if I look like Romvos, the man who offered me
to the goddess. You can find his name on the **inscription** at the base.

Can you decipher the letters? They are Greek but belong
to the era archaeologists call Archaic. That period extends
from 600 to 480 BC.

the athenian trireme

Nine men are leaning over the oars. It is with the force of their strong arms that they make the ship move.

They are **oarsmen** on a trireme. Do you think they could be on Paralos – the **trireme** used for the official missions of the Athenian state? Most of their fellow-oarsmen have disappeared. Not during a **sea-battle**, but when this, the **relief** depicting them, was destroyed.

How can archaeologists be sure that these oarsmen are actually on a trireme although the relief is incomplete? Well... archaeologists are very good at finding clues. Not only did they find 2 of the missing pieces on the Acropolis but they also discovered, while searching the collections of other museums, a piece in Italy and a drawing – based on a copy of the original – in the British Museum, London. The relief itself was discovered by the French archaeologist François Lenormant in the 19th century.

In those days, if you went south to the port of Piraeus, and walked around a neosoikos –a **ship-shed**– you would have seen the Athenians pulling the triremes ashore for repair. A trireme was made of fir and oak wood.
It was about 35 metres **long**, **narrow and shallow-draught**
with pledget and wax sealed seams.
It had a **movable** mast that was taken off for battles,
a large **square sail** and a smaller one at the bow.
Attached to the ship's prow was a bronze **beak** used to ram enemy ships.
A trireme had 170 oars set in **three rows**, one on top of the other,
and turned with two steering wheels, one on each side of the stern.
Two large eyes were painted on both sides of the bow
so that the ships could look ahead and easily find their way at sea.

a warship
easy
to
manoeuvre

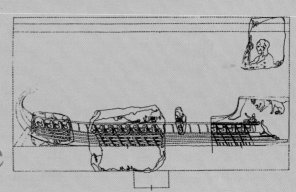

The crew
The **trierarch** commanded the ship with the help of his officers.
The **boatswain** set the rhythm for the oarsmen with the help of a
flute-player.
The **proreus**, the **look out officer**, watched the weather,
the winds and the currents and kept the steersman informed.
The **steward** took care of provisions on the ship.
The **sailors** handled the sails.
The **marines** were ready to attack.
All together there were 210-216 men on board.

the Athenian athlete

I would like to participate in the **Panathenaic Games** that will take place
at the end of this summer, in the month of Hekatombaion,
when we celebrate the **birthday** of the goddess Athena.

Euthymides –the pot-painter– drew my portrait on the clay
plate I will dedicate to the goddess.

The **Panathenaia** is the **greatest festival** of our city. We celebrate it
every 4 years.
It involves religious ceremonies, a **great procession**, and sacrifices to honour
the goddess. Besides this, we have musical and athletic contests.
Many friends of mine will compete in **horse races**, **running**, **torch races**,
and **rowing** competitions held at Piraeus.

I am a hoplitodromos, that is, an **armed runner**. The race I run requires
an **excellent physical condition**:
not only do I have to run over **two stadia**[6], but I also have to
carry a shield and javelin while doing so.

If I win, I will be awarded pots filled with oil from the sacred olive trees
of the goddess.
This is the prize given to the winners of Panathenaia by the city.

We call the pots **Panathenaic amphoras**.
On one side, under the figure of **Athena Promachos** –meaning
"Athena who leads in battle"– the inscription reads "From the games
of Athens".
The scene depicted on the back, shows which **competition**
was won by the athlete.

The Graces personified grace, beauty and joy. They passed their time accompanying Athena and Aphrodite, frolicking in the open air together with Dionysos, dancing to the sound of Apollo's lyre...

the Graces

To begin, the sculptor would **choose** a piece of marble **suitably sized**
for his work.
He might have **drawn** the representation on the stone to use it as a **guide**.

Next, with **chisel** and **hammer**, he would **carve off** the marble around
the figures to produce a rough approximation of their shapes. He would then
use **finer, toothed chisels** to work on the details. Finally, he would **smooth**
the surface of the relief with **emery** and paint his work.

Here, you can clearly see the figures projecting out from the stone. Who are
these girls carved on the relief dancing to the tune of the flute? Are they the
Graces, the graceful, beautiful daughters of Zeus and the Oceanid Eurynome?

Are they Euphrosyne, Thaleia and Aglaia? **Maybe...**

How about the little boy at the end of the line dancing with them?
Is it **Erichthonios**, the mythical son of the goddess Athena?

Archaeologists can only speculate about these identities, although Pausanias
–the travel-writer– did write about a **shrine** of the Graces on the Acropolis.

who
is
who

Your biggest clue is his legs...

She is accompanied
by her favourite bird...

Look carefully at what he is wearing...

puzzle

Most of the ancient objects you come across upon entering a museum are the victims of time; the pots, the sculptures, the statues, the reliefs...
In other words, they may have broken to pieces and their fragments either seriously damaged or completely destroyed.
How do archaeologists **identify** each object? How do they date it?
And how do they attribute the fragments?

Each object is like a puzzle!

Sometimes **archaeologists** actually put the pieces together in exactly the same way you do with a puzzle.
Sometimes they study **descriptions** of the object written when it was still in one piece.
They may also uncover **copies** made in later historical periods.
They may even figure out to which object a fragment belongs by combining information from **history** and **mythology**,
the **place** in which it was found,
the **monument** to which it lies close,
the **material** of which it is made,
an **inscription** carved on the stone,
and, if they are lucky, the **signature** of the **artist** who created it.

If you look closely at these works... you can always find something to tell you **who is who**!

41

the Sphinx
a mythical creature

A mythical creature,
a beautiful **female head** with hair that reaches her shoulders,
a creature with the body and limbs of a **lion**
and the **wings** of a bird...
It is the Sphinx **smiling** at us.
Is she smiling because you are looking at her **wondering** what she is?

She was the sister of Kerberos, Lernaia Hydra and other **monstrous creatures**
born to Echidna and Typhon, monsters themselves.
She is the one who asked **riddles** to unsuspecting travelers
in order to decide if they could gain the right of passage through the gates
of **Thebes**:
"Which creature goes on four legs in the morning, on two at mid-day and
on three in the evening?"
"**Man**" answered **King Oedipus**, the only person to solve the riddle.
Since then all the travelers have been safe to pass.

The Acropolis Sphinx stood on a tall column.
It was a **votive offering** to the goddess.
It was probably meant to remind people of the old
chthonic divinities of fertility and death that they used
to worship before the Olympian gods.

**The smile on her lips
is typical of the
Archaic period statues.**

the young rider

This statue of a young **horse-rider** is one of many dedicated to the goddess Athena.

You can tell that he has **broken into pieces**. Many of these are **missing**.

If you take a close look, you will notice that his head is not made of marble! It is plaster.

His head was found ten years later than his **body** and followed a different path. The body stayed in Athens, while the head was bought by a **collector**, Georges Rampin, who donated it to the Louvre Museum in Paris.

On the inscription you can read the name archaeologists gave him: the **Rampin Rider**, after the collector to whom his head once belonged.

When archaeologists were **certain** that body and head **matched**, they **completed** the statue adding this **plaster copy** of the original head. We don't know his name... The **wreath** on his head suggests that he may be an **athlete**; a champion horse racer.

Many **fragmentary statues of riders** are exhibited in the New Acropolis Museum.

You can see their heads, torsos and thighs along with the horses they rode. In ancient Athens, 'hippeis', or riders, were the second highest of the four classes set out by Solon[7] and therefore many Athenians liked being represented as riders.

Her name is Peploforos. She is wearing a peplos[8], a dress tied around the waist with an ornamented belt. She has a wreath on her long, wavy hair and wears earrings.

Tall and slender, in a long dress decorated with meanders and drapery clinging to her body and revealing her legs as she takes a small step forward. Look at the sandals on her feet, her well-shaped nails and her long, thick hair done in an elaborate style.

Over her shoulders, she has thrown a himation.

beautiful
Korai

The Athenians had **dedicated** over 200 Korai to the goddess Athena. When the shrines on the Acropolis were destroyed by the Persians, the inhabitants buried the wounded Korai in a groove of the rock near the Erechtheion. In 1886, after many centuries in the dark, 14 Korai saw the light of day again, when they were discovered by archaeologists excavating the area.

The heavy drapes of her himation and the embossed patterns of her peplos complement her well-shaped body.

She is Chiotissa, the woman from Chios in glamorous dress.

Athena

Athena wearing the aegis, a breastplate made of goatskin and decorated with snake heads, extends her left arm menacingly towards Engelados and chases him to Sicily where she throws the whole island onto his body... crushing him.

Engelados' body is missing. Only his foot is left behind to remind us of him. But we know it is Engelados, because mythology books tell us so. Further on, to his right, another giant lies wounded.

A huge Athena, **defeating the giant Engelados**, was carved
on Parian marble on the east pediment of the ancient temple
destroyed by the Persians.
It is part of a scene from **Gigantomachy**, the battle between
the gods and the **Giants** –the sons of Gaia and Uranus–
who wanted to usurp the absolute power of the gods.
The **Olympian** gods under Zeus and Athena, goddess of battle,
fought back and triumphed.

the war goddess

Athena's statue has been heavily damaged.
Archaeologists gathered the pieces they could find and, after studying
the head and body posture, filled in the missing parts and reconstructed
the statue to its original form.

Fallen giants complete the other half of the pediment.

49

what work do they do?

A scribe with a framed reddish plate on his knees.

A bearded man sits on a **stool**.
He has a flat object on his lap.
Perhaps he was a **scribe** – a profession
which is now extinct.
In **Classical Athens**, many citizens knew
how to read and write.
Girls were taught to write at home by their mothers
or tutors.
Boys, on the other hand,
would go to a teacher's school to learn.
Ancient Athenians wrote on clay
or **waxed tablets** and **fragments of pots**.
They wrote with bone or metal **styluses**,
which looked like big nails.
With these they would **carve** letters
and words onto the clay and wax.
If they made a mistake on the wax,
they could correct it by pressing down
with the flat end of the stylus.
But who are these two scribes dedicated,
among others, to Athena?
Perhaps they were **secretaries** who wrote
down the resolutions of Parliament
and the Assembly of the City.

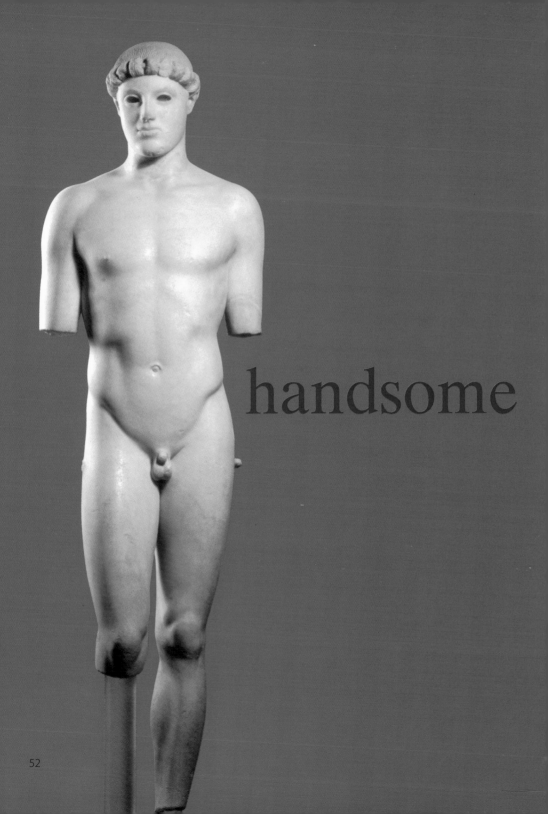

handsome

young men

The ancient Greeks believed that, in men, both **beauty**
and **ethos** –moral standards–
were revealed through a toned, **athletic** body.
That is why **all young men** are represented in the **nude**.
The **Kritias Boy** (so called because he is attributed to the **sculptor** Kritias)
is the statue of a young athlete probably completed before 480 BC.
He looks so alive!
He is **posing** for the sculptor with his head slightly tilted to the right
and his well-kempt, **tightly braided hair**
wrapped around his head.
His legs are strong but his feet **barely touch** the ground
giving the impression of **movement**.
What do you think the expression of his eyes would have been
when the **pupils**, which were made separately, were inlaid
in the now empty sockets?
What **colour** might they have been?

When you approach the statues, you can detect
traces of colour in the pores of the stone.
Hair, eyebrows, eyes, mouths and clothes
were all painted.

**A similar hair style is worn
by the unknown youth
they have called the Blond Ephebos
– the blond adolescent.
Why did they call him that? Because they
found traces of yellow colour on his hair.
The colour of his eyes, however,
has faded away.**

silent Athena

The relief of silent Athena was found near the Parthenon in 1888.
We do not know **who** created it, but we have a rough idea of **when** it was created.
It was sometime between 470 and 460 BC. A time when sculpture workshops
in Attica were very busy and sculptors worked long hours.
The danger of a Persian invasion was now over, and the citizens made
votive offerings to the gods to thank them for their part in the victory.

Athena tilts her head slightly to the left resting her chin on her shoulder.
She is serious, without even the hint of a smile.
Her **helmet** does not seem to weigh her down.
A **peplos** enfolds her whole body.
Her right hand rests on her waist.
Her left foot is set firmly on the ground.
The toes of her right foot barely touch the earth.
The **spear** pointing downwards supports her weight.

Is she sad?
Is she deep in thought?
What might she be thinking of?
Is something bothering her?
Or is she simply resting?
Perhaps she stoops to **read** the inscription on the **stele** next to her.

**We will never know what the sculptor intended by
giving her that expression!
What do you think?**

the Karyatides

One Karyatid is missing!
Lord Elgin had it removed in 1803 and it is now in the British Museum,
along with the other sculptures from the Acropolis.

Six female figures –Korai– made of Pentelic marble, support on their heads
the roof of the **prostasis** – the small terrace on the south side of the
Erechtheion, where **King Kekrop's** tomb was believed to be.
Each figure wears a **Doric peplos**, falling in smooth **folds**,
and has her long hair tied in **two pleats** crossing over on her back.
She carries a basket on her head.
She has one foot forward for better balance.

To the Athenians the figures were simply known as "the Korai".
Karyatides –the name by which they are known today–
was given later.
Perhaps they are the maidens who served in the temple
of Artemis Karyatis, at Karyes in the Peloponnese. Maybe...
There are many legends.
We also come across Karyatides in the Delphi shrine where they
decorate the Sifnian and Knidian thesauruses.
They can also be found in Roman copies and even
at neo-classic houses of later periods.

they are columns, actually!

The Karyatides are columns,
like the elegant Ionic columns of Erechtheion and the temple
of Athena Nike, with **volutes**[9] decorating their **capitals**[10],
or like the Doric columns of the Parthenon and the Propylaia.

Ancient artists were greatly inspired by nature.
The Ionic volute resembles a fern sprouting in spring, while
the Corinthian capital is embraced by the wide leaves of an **acanthus**,
as in the temple of **Olympian Zeus**,
near the Gate of Adrianus.

the Parthenon
frieze...
a comic strip carved on marble

Imagine visiting the Acropolis with your friends 2,500 years ago.
You go through the Propylaia to the Parthenon.
You are captivated by the lively scenes represented on the **west pediment**.
You walk on and stand behind the tall columns of the temple.
You look up. Now you see a long **procession** moving slowly.
Hundreds of faces: women, girls, children, young men, old men, riders, animals...
It is the Panathenaic procession carved by **Pheidias** and his **apprentices**
on the **Parthenon frieze**.
The procession starts at the southwest corner of the Parthenon
where it **splits** in two and continues to the east.
You walk north-east. Your friends walk in the opposite direction.
You meet again at the entrance of the Parthenon, on the east side
of the temple, where **all the participants of the festival meet**.
High above, the gods sit and watch the **King Archon**[11] **receive**
the newly-woven peplos for the goddess Athena.

Today you see the Parthenon from the **Parthenon Room** of the New Museum. It
stands on the top of the rock, gleaming come rain or shine...

Have you noticed that some of the frieze slabs are not made from marble? The
marble ones used to stand on the Parthenon columns before they were taken to
the **British Museum**. Therefore, some of the slabs you see today are plaster cast
copies of the originals.

The Parthenon had 92 metopes. Most of them have been destroyed. On statues and figures carved in relief, they would attach bronze decorative ornaments, jewels, wreaths and weapons glittering in the sun.

colour
everywhere

Today, if someone asks what the marble statues and temples look like, the first thing that springs to mind is that they have the **colour of the material** of which they are made. They are white – although the marble is no longer as bright and translucent as it once was.

But if you lived in antiquity, when the monuments were new, you would have a completely different **impression**. Because back then, everything was in **colour**!

All the **decorative elements** of the buildings were painted. Only the columns and the walls remained white. Everything else had **colour**: the capitals, the friezes, the pediments, the metopes, the roof panels, the cornices...

Ancient artists used only a few colours: deep crimson, red, blue, yellow, green and gold. They used **natural colours** – prepared with minerals and rocks containing colour, or with plant and animal dye.

Until the 5th century, at least, painters used **block colours**, with neither hues nor shades.
Today, their works would appear too brightly coloured to us. In those days, however, it made sense to use bright colours at the **top** of high buildings – so they could be seen from a **distance**.

The pediments, of which each temple has two, are the triangles formed under the roof and over the narrow sides of the building. A pediment is called aetoma in Greek, meaning 'eagle', because it looks like the spread wings of an eagle.

the birth of Athena

Zeus sits on his **throne**. On either side of him stand the **Olympian gods**.
At the far end, on the left, stands the sun-god Helios in his chariot.
On the far right, stands the moon-goddess Selene.
What are they waiting for?
They are waiting for Hephaestus to put an end to the headache tormenting Zeus,
the father of gods and men.
Hephaestus cracked **open the head** of Zeus with an axe and out came
his daughter Athena in **full armour**.
The goddess Athena wore a helmet, held a shield and a spear
and looked ready to fight.
What had happened?
When **Metis** – the beautiful Titanid – was pregnant with Zeus' child,
Mother Earth prophesized she would give birth to a girl. But Mother Earth also
foretold that Metis' second child would be a boy. And that boy would be so
strong that he would battle his father and **take the throne**, just like Zeus
had done before him. So Zeus **swallowed** both Metis
and his unborn daughter to prevent any child being born from her.

The pediments are triangular, about 28m long and up to 3.45m high and decorated with 50 figures. The central figures are carved in the upright position, while those at the sides sit or lie to fit the triangular shape.

the name of the city

In the (very) olden days, the inhabitants of each city looked for
a **protector god**. When the time came for the **citizens** of **Kekropia** to decide,
Poseidon and **Athena** competed to be protector of their city by offering gifts.
Poseidon offered a **horse** –like those who pulled his golden chariot
on the waves– and a **spring** of sea water.
But the people of Kekropia preferred a different gift;
the **olive tree** that Athena gave them. A tree that
provided them with **food**, oil balm for their wounds and wood to keep them
warm.
So the city was called **Athena**...
Poseidon was furious and sent waves to flood the plane of Eleusis.
Despite the suffering he caused them,
the Athenians **respected** the god of the sea,
because they needed him to **protect** their **ships** from storms and tempests.
Athenians claimed there was **evidence of the contest** inside
the Erechtheion, the holiest temple of the Acropolis. They claimed that the hole
in the ground had been made by Poseidon's trident and that Athena's holy tree
was still in place.

INITIATIVE FOR THE RETURN OF THE MARBLES

Resolution for the return of the Parthenon marbles

80% of British citizens favour the return of the marbles

The Australians demand that the Parthenon sculptures be returned

International campaign for the return of the marbles

INTERNET RALLY FOR THE RETURN OF THE MARBLES

BRITISH OLYMPIAN CHAMPIONS IN FAVOUR OF THE RETURN OF THE MARBLES

the Acropolis marbles...

In the old days, before Greece became an independent state, there were **no laws for the protection of antiquities**. Therefore it was fairly easy for travelers, antiquity lovers and illicit dealers to take Greek antiquities to the museums of their own countries.

The sculptures of the Acropolis were a spectacular target!

far from home

The largest and most important collection of works of art from the Acropolis is exhibited in the **British Museum**, London. They were removed from the Acropolis and sold to that museum by Lord Elgin.

In 1799, **Lord Elgin** was appointed **ambassador** of Great Britain to the High Gate – the Ottoman Court in Istanbul. He sought and gained permission to send craftsmen to Athens –under Ottoman rule at the time– to **draw sketches** of the monuments and **make casts** for the decoration of his stately home in Scotland.

However, from 1801 to 1804, Elgin's men did more than sketch and make casts of the monuments: they actually **tore off an important part** of the Parthenon's decorative sculpture, reliefs from the Athena Nike temple, a Karyatid from the Erechtheion, a capital, a column drum...

The Parthenon	Athens	London
Slabs from the frieze	40	56
Metopes	48	15
28 figures (still intact) from pediments	9	19

Greece insists that the sculptures **be returned** so that the **unity** of the monument can be restored and all the works can be displayed together, here in the New Acropolis Museum.

Michalis Photiadis, the architectural spirit of the museum, says:

The New Acropolis Museum is a universal cultural asset. Thirty-five years and four competitions –two national and two international– preceded the allocation of this project to a developer. Those of us who participated had to deal with a number of issues, starting with the problem of the site. Three sites were initially considered...

In 2000, after the site at Makrigiannis had been selected, the final international competition was held. It took into account the changes that had occurred at the site, resulting from the construction of the new underground station and archaeological excavations in the area. This site is ideal for visitors who wish to come to the museum to learn, study, and gather information before going up to the Acropolis, or vice versa. As you can see, the museum is wedged among the city buildings... It would have been nice to have a big open site. However this was simply not possible if the museum was to be near the monument, right in the centre of Athens.

Constructing a museum is a complex project. The winning design team was an international one with Photiadis' offices in Athens and Bernard Tschumi's in New York. A vast amount of people were involved! We collaborated with civil engineers, mechanical engineers, archaeologists, geotechnical consultants, seismologists, interior designers, specialists in fire safety, acoustics and lighting, graphic designers, museum consultants, legal advisors, landscape architects, transportation engineers, etc. There were about sixty specialist consultants in all, ready to tackle any problem, big or small.

The New Acropolis Museum was not built as merely an inert host to the antiquities. The hundreds of visitors and employees that walk around make it a living organism. It has 14,000 sq m of exhibition space, two snack bars, several gift shops, a restaurant, a kitchen, an auditorium, an amphitheatre,

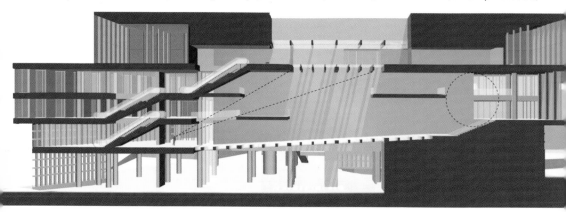

A section of the New Museum: The light from the Parthenon Room goes all the way down to the ancient Athenian neighbourhoods.

seating areas, temporary exhibitions... On the four lowest levels there are workshops, store rooms, a garage, a mechanical room and other auxiliary areas covering about 23,000 sq m in total. We designed the museum in a way that would allow a whole family to happily pass an entire day here.

We started by walking around the area where the New Museum was to be built in order to determine how the building should stand in relation to its surrounding environment. There were a number of factors to consider: the maximum permissible height, site coverage, overall area in square meters, distances from neighbouring buildings, etc. These factors determined the exact position of the museum, ensuring the visitor a clear view of the monument. Furthermore, the whole area around the Acropolis is full of antiquities. Before we could start digging for the foundations, excavations took place revealing layers of dwellings from various periods. It was decided that we should keep three of those: The Hellenistic (circa 2nd century BC), the Roman (3rd-4th century AD) and the Byzantine ones (4th-7th century AD). The evidence of roads and houses proves that Athenians have continuously inhabited the area next to the Acropolis. If we were to dig deeper we would find tokens from even earlier periods.

Our central idea was to have the Parthenon Room on the top floor covered with glass, allowing the visitor to see the Panathenaic Procession on the frieze surrounding the Parthenon. For this to be fully effective, we had to turn the axis of the room in such a way that the light would hit the frieze from the same angle it did when Pheidias created it. The Parthenon frieze stood right at the top of the four marble walls of the temple, at a height of 10.30m – higher than a three storey building. Standing between the Doric columns, the frieze was part of the soul of the temple and could be seen clearly only by the gods. Now, we have brought it down to the level of the mortal gaze, at a height of 1.50m.

We used plain, simple, contemporary materials. The structural frame of the building – columns, beams and slabs– is made of concrete, visible both on the inside and outside of the museum, serving as a background to the exhibits. The glass frames are made of steel. Glass plays an important role throughout the museum: it is used to separate the rooms, and, furthermore, it is used on the floors to provide a continuous, unobstructed view from the Parthenon Room at the top, all the way down to the underground excavations of ancient Athens. The floors are marble: black Macedonian marble is used in the common rooms and corridors, and reddish ochre from mount Elikon is used elsewhere, to match the patina of the sculptures. The building was designed to withstand a 10 Richter earthquake, though no earthquake over 8 Richter has ever occurred in the area. In fact, no earthquakes have ever threatened the Parthenon seriously. Adopting the method of our remarkable ancestors, we smoothed the marble of the rock to allow the monuments to "slide", thus resisting the potential damage posed by an earthquake.
Can there be a greater satisfaction for an architect than to be involved in the creation of such a project next to the Acropolis?

Endnotes

1. The **metopes** are the (usually) decorated slabs around a Doric temple, found above the columns.
2. The **frieze** is the ornamented horizontal part of an Ionic temple that lies between the architrave (directly on top of the capital) and the cornice (the projecting element of the roof).
3. The **panathenaic amphora** is a large vase given as a prize to the winners of the Panathenaic Games.
4. The **pediment** is the triangular structure that surmounts the façade of the temple (typically) supported by columns and decorated with reliefs and sculpture.
5. A **himation** was made of thick woolen fabric and was worn by both men and women usually as a coat.
6. A **stadium** equals 185 metres approximately, so they had to run about 370 metres.
7. **Solon** was an Athenian law maker and poet (one of the Seven Sages of Greece) who reformed the class system dividing the population into 4 classes.
8. A **peplos** was a woman's dress made of woolen fabric. Before wrapping it around their body, they would fold it in two to create an overfold. They would then fasten it at either shoulder with the help of brooch-like pins that attached the back of the dress to the front.
9. The **volute** is the spiral scroll-shaped decorative element on the top of the Ionic capital.
10. The **capital** is the crowning element, the top of a column.
11. **King Archon** was the title of the official of the Athenian state responsible for religious affairs.

Further reading for young people

Connolly, Peter (1998) *The Ancient City. Life in Classical Athens and Rome*. Oxford: Oxford University Press.
Hatziaslani, Kornilia (2004) *Promenades at the Parthenon*. Athens: Kastaniotis (CD).
Royer, Sophie, Catherine Sales & François Trassard, (2003) *La Vie des Grecs au Temps de Périklès*. Paris: Larousse.
Roberts, Jennifer T. & Tracy Barrett, (2004) *The Ancient World*. Oxford & New York: Oxford University Press.

General bibliography

Boardman, J., N. G. L. Hammond, D. M. Lewis, M. Ostwald, J. K. Davies and
S. Hornhblower (eds) (1988)
The Cambridge Ancient History, volume 3, Cambridge University Press.
Cook, R.M. (1986) *Greek Art*. London: Penguin.
Graves, R. (1955) *The Greek Myths*. London: Penguin.
Jones, W.H.S. (ed.) (1966) *Pausanias, Description of Greece*. Book I (Attica and Corinth).
Loeb Classical Library.
Cambridge, MA.: Harvard University Press.
Korres, M. (1993) *From Pentelicon to the Parthenon*. Athens: Melissa.
Richter, G. (1969) *A Handbook of Greek Art*. London: Phaidon.

Websites

http://www.newacropolismuseum.gr
http://odysseus.culture.gr
http://www.culture.gr

Writing a book is an adventure, not only for the author but also for those
near and dear, who listen to his/her thoughts, read and re-read the text.
For me, these are my boys, Orestis and Leon, my companion Benny,
Michalis Photiadis, the architectural spirit of the museum, and Panos
Valavanis, companion to my archaeological quests. I thank them all.

MdC

Picture Credits

p. 14, Propylaia © Ministry of Culture • Archaeological Receipts Fund
p. 16, Temple of Athena Nike © Ministry of Culture • Archaeological Receipts Fund
p. 20, Parthenon © Ministry of Culture • Archaeological Receipts Fund
p. 22, Erechtheion © Ministry of Culture • Archaeological Receipts Fund
p. 26, Acr. 1347 © 1st Ephorate of Prehistoric and Classical Antiquities • Ministry of Culture
    • Archaeological Receipts Fund
p. 28-29, Acr. 35-36 © 1st Ephorate of Prehistoric and Classical Antiquities • Ministry of Culture
    • Archaeological Receipts Fund
p. 30, Acr. 701 © Ministry of Culture • Archaeological Receipts Fund
p. 32-33, Acr. 624 © 1st Ephorate of Prehistoric and Classical Antiquities • Ministry of Culture
    • Archaeological Receipts Fund
p. 34, Acr. 1339 © Ministry of Culture • Archaeological Receipts Fund • Ministry of Culture
    • Archaeological Receipts Fund
p. 36, Acr. 67 © 1st Ephorate of Prehistoric and Classical Antiquities • Ministry of Culture • Archaeological Receipts Fund
p. 38, Acr. 702 © Ministry of Culture • Archaeological Receipts Fund
p. 40, Acr. 12981, Acr. 1345, Acr. 638 © 1st Ephorate of Prehistoric and Classical Antiquities • Ministry of Culture
    • Archaeological Receipts Fund
p. 42, Acr. 630 © Ministry of Culture • Archaeological Receipts Fund
p. 44, Acr. 590 © Ministry of Culture • Archaeological Receipts Fund
p. 46-47, Acr. 679, Acr. 682, Acr. 671, Acr. 675 © Ministry of Culture • Archaeological Receipts Fund
p. 47, Acr. 684 © 1st Ephorate of Prehistoric and Classical Antiquities • Ministry of Culture
    • Archaeological Receipts Fund
p. 48-49, Acr. 631 © 1st Ephorate of Prehistoric and Classical Antiquities • Ministry of Culture
    • Archaeological Receipts Fund
p. 50-51, Acr. 144, Acr. 629 © 1st Ephorate of Prehistoric and Classical Antiquities • Ministry of Culture
    • Archaeological Receipts Fund
p. 52, Acr. 698 © 1st Ephorate of Prehistoric and Classical Antiquities • Ministry of Culture
    • Archaeological Receipts Fund
p. 53, Acr. 689 © Ministry of Culture • Archaeological Receipts Fund
p. 54, Acr. 695 © Ministry of Culture • Archaeological Receipts Fund
p. 56, Erechtheion © Ministry of Culture • Archaeological Receipts Fund
p. 57, Acr. 15000 © 1st Ephorate of Prehistoric and Classical Antiquities • Ministry of Culture
    • Archaeological Receipts Fund
p. 58, Acr. 857, Acr. 860, Acr. 864, Acr. 865, Acr. 868 © Ministry of Culture • Archaeological Receipts Fund
p. 58, 9th slab of the west frieze, 12th slab of the west frieze, Acr. 877 © 1st Ephorate of Prehistoric
    and Classical Antiquities • Ministry of Culture • Archaeological Receipts Fund
p. 62, Reconstruction of the east pediment of the Parthenon © 1st Ephorate of Prehistoric and Classical Antiquities •
Ministry of Culture • Archaeological Receipts Fund
p. 63, Reconstruction of the west pediment of the Parthenon © 1st Ephorate of Prehistoric and Classical Antiquities
    • Ministry of Culture • Archaeological Receipts Fund

The sketches on pages 10, 11, 12, 13 and 60 are by Stamatis Bonatsos.
The sketch on page 18 is by Manolis Korres from his book *From Pentelicon to the Parthenon.* (1992) Athens: Melissa.
The sketch on page 35 is by L. Beschi from Ismene Trianti's book *To Mouseio Akropoleos.* (1998)
    Athens: Eurobank (in Greek).
The reconstruction of the east and the west pediment of the Parthenon (p. 62-63) is by K. Schwerzek from Ismene
    Trianti's book *To Mouseio Akropoleos.* (1998) Athens: Eurobank (in Greek).
The sketch on page 66 is by Michalis Photiadis.
Our warmest thanks to all of them.